Counsellors in the course of their practice are likely to come across clients with particular difficulties, such as experience of incest, drug or alcohol addiction, or eating difficulties. These issues may not be the main focus of the counselling and it may not be appropriate to refer the client on to a specialist in one of these fields, if such exists locally. There may be literature available but little guidance for the counsellor seeking it.

The Publications Sub-Committee of the British Association for Counselling are publishing a series of booklets to help counsellors in this situation. Written by specialist counsellors or therapists, they draw attention to issues which are likely to arise for the client and for the counsellor and which may be missed by the novice. They also provide a guide to the relevant literature. Being brief, readable and to the point it is hoped that counsellors will be able to consult them even when time and money are short. In this way it is hoped that these booklets will contribute to the raising of standards of counselling in general.

The Sub-Committee would like to thank not only those members who worked to produce these booklets, but also Isobel Palmer and Sally Cook, and the consultant editors, myself, Gladeana McMahon and Stephen Palmer, whose contribution was vital.

Julia Segal
Chair, Publications Sub-Committee of the
British Association for Counselling from 1987 to 1993.

Sheila Naish

Sheila Naish is a retired social worker who has spent 13 years in the field of adoption and fostering. With her partner, Joe, she runs a small bed and breakfast establishment in the Pennines, catering mainly for cyclists and walkers doing the Pennine Way.

She still does occasional sessional work for Bradford Social Services, together with some private counselling. She is setting up a support network for women who have undergone reconstructive vaginal surgery and undertakes voluntary counselling for the new Yorkshire & Humberside After Adoption Service in Leeds.

Counselling People with

Infertility Problems

Sheila Naish

British Association for Counselling
1 Regent Place • Rugby • Warwickshire CV21 2PJ
Office 01788 550899 • Information Line 01788 578328 • Fax 01788 562189

© **BAC 1994**   **ISBN 0 946181 45 4**

Poetry excerpts taken from *For a Child Expected* by **Ann Ridler**, published by Carcanet Press Ltd. in *Nine Bright Shiners*.

Published by	British Association for Counselling, 1 Regent Place, Rugby, Warwickshire CV21 2PJ
First printed 1994	
Produced by	BAC, company limited by guarantee 2175320 registered in England & Wales, and registered charity 298361
Printed by	Quorn Litho, Queens Road, Loughborough, Leicestershire LE11 1HH

Others in the series

Counselling Adults who were Abused as Children by Peter Dale
Counselling People in Eating Distress by Carole Waskett

British Association for Counselling

- Codes of Ethics & Practice for Counsellors, for Counselling Skills, for Trainers and for the Supervision of Counsellors
- Counselling publications mail order service
- Quarterly journal with in-depth articles, news and views of members
- Individual accreditation, supervisor recognition and counsellor training course recognition schemes

Join BAC now — the Voice of Counselling

Details of the above and much more besides:
BAC, 1 Regent Place, Rugby CV21 2PJ. Tel: 01788 550899

Contents

Foreword

Approximately one couple in six will consult their Doctor because of their inability to conceive at some time in their life. Approximately one couple in ten have no children, and a little over half of these are involuntarily childless.

Health is not merely the absence of disease but includes also the opportunity to fulfil one's dreams. For most of us, nothing can impede our dreams as much as being infertile. Infertility is a common and devastating problem.

However, infertility does not seem to have a high claim on resources. Neither National Health Services nor insurance schemes recognise the immense suffering from infertility in their funding priorities. Ideally, people should not have children they don't want and should be able to have the children they do want. Family planning and fertility services should go hand in hand. However, the former are well funded and the latter very poorly funded.

Witgenstein said that the philosopher's job was to hold the world in a different way, so that people could see issues afresh and perhaps judge them differently. I have been campaigning for many years to sensitise the public to the silent agony of subfertile couples. Some years ago I received notoriety by stating my belief that the infertility services should compete more successfully with other 'curative' services, even if this meant longer waiting lists for painful and debilitating elective surgical procedures. I stand absolutely behind what I said then.

I certainly wish to change public perceptions about the moral relevance of whether or not infertility is a disease. There is no moral relevance to this distinction as far as the distribution of scarce resources is concerned. Disease is not an evil in itself, it is the suffering that disease causes which is an evil. It therefore follows that if greater suffering is caused by a condition which is not classified as a disease, then that condition should have the higher claim for resources.

When people pay their health tax they seem to do so for three reasons. First, and most important, they regard their health tax as a form of insurance. People who are not worried about their fertility or who have already had children will not give assisted conception services much weight under this category. Secondly, people wish to contribute towards health services as a form of public good from which neither they nor anybody else can be excluded and from which everybody stands to benefit. Vaccination comes under this category. Lastly, people contribute out of a sense of altruism—sometimes called the principle of rescue. Infertility services seem to have to rely on this last (and apparently weakest) motivation for the contribution towards health.

That infertility causes immense personal suffering can hardly be denied. The extent to which people will jeopardise their financial security in order to purchase infertility treatment serves as the most powerful 'cost benefit analysis'.

Sheila Naish is to be congratulated for bringing the private agony of infertility out into the open. She deals perceptively with the Health Service implications of this complex condition and the complex interaction between Health Services Management, medical detail and the emotions of subfertile people. The rage, guilt, depression and isolation that couples feel are described from the perspective by a counsellor with deep personal knowledge of the suffering of individuals.

This is an important booklet and I wish it every success.

Professor Richard J. Lilford
Professor in Obstetrics & Gynaecology
The General Infirmary, Leeds

Introduction

The most dramatic successes or failures of infertility treatment regularly make the news by focusing on the sensational. But when you come face to face with a client with a fertility problem, you are likely to feel as dissatisfied by the semi-medical handbooks provided for a lay readership as by the emotive snippets of misinformation in the popular press.

This guidebook is written with the aim of giving enough information on the causes of infertility and the procedures and treatments carried out in clinics to enable the generic counsellor to understand and work with clients with this problem.

The emotional and ethical aspects of infertility raise many issues for both the counsellor and the client.

The experience of infertility colours everything—whatever issue brings client and counsellor together in the first place will be profoundly affected, distorted even, when there is also a fertility problem. Infertility affects the capacity to function in close relationships, socially and at work, permeating every aspect of life. It may stop work on other problems which have to go on 'hold' for the time being.

Counselling People with Infertility Problems

Lovers whose lifted hands are candles in winter,
Whose gentle ways like streams in the easy summer,
Lying together
For secret setting of a child, love what they do,
Thinking they make that candle immortal,
                              those streams forever flow,
And yet do better than they know.......

from *For a Child Expected* by **Ann Ridler**

The figures[†]

Humans are the least fertile animals. In Western societies one couple in six will be infertile. Of the remaining five, 80% will achieve a pregnancy in the first year of trying, 20% within the second year. The 'causes' of infertility are roughly: 40% male, 40% female, 20% joint factors, so the problem is common enough. The 'success rates' announced for different treatments have the dubious accuracy of hire purchase interest rates, but it is a fact that less than one fifth of those undergoing treatment ever manage to conceive.

Normal expectations

Considering what a common experience it is, society provides little preparation for infertility. 'Pronatalism' is the assumption that parenthood is both a right and a duty, and all societies are pronatalist. From the first game of 'Mummies and Daddies' onwards, parenthood is seen as one rung on the ladder to maturity and fulfilment.

The pressure exists from birth. All cultures and religions enjoin their members to increase and multiply. The question 'Why children?' is still an uncomfortable one. Workshops on 'Shall I have Children?' fail to recruit enough participants. The small proportion of people making an informed decision to remain childfree are often labelled odd, 'selfish', 'materialistic', 'career-minded'.

[†] See page 54

Fertility for all is assumed. Tradition first, formal sex education later, place the emphasis on avoiding unwanted pregnancy. Most children grow to adulthood with these prohibitions ringing in their ears. Apart from a small proportion of individuals with a known medical problem, we all take it for granted that if we want a family, children will come along when the time is right.

What is infertility?

Sociologically and medically infertility is the failure of a woman to achieve pregnancy/carry a child to term, or of a man to cause pregnancy—a failure not to be taken seriously until after one year of regular, unprotected sexual intercourse. In the UK it is now the biggest single reason for referrals to gynaecologists.

But there are also individuals who are childless—voluntarily or involuntarily—whose grief and pain may be no less than those mentioned above, and for whom childlessness is a lifelong condition with many of the features of infertility. Much of the material in this booklet will also apply to them.

For there is not always a clear dividing line between those who choose to have children and those who do not. Some may suspect infertility, but for a wide range of reasons choose not to expose themselves to investigation. What about people in homosexual relationships, the single, the disabled (who are sometimes warned unnecessarily about the risks of producing children because of the high costs to the taxpayer)?

There are people who know there are genetic risks to the child, or health risks for themselves; individuals with partners who have 'enough' children from previous relationships, individuals with partners who don't want children. They may be said to have chosen childlessness, but by default. It can be the cause of deep personal anguish nevertheless, remedies differ.

No choice whatsoever is available to the small group of men and women born without the necessary equipment. They have at least the small advantage that they will have had more preparation for the disappointment of childlessness. Their lives can be spent protecting their secret in a society which gives credits for sexuality.

Infertility is a medical condition, but can be an emotional state, a life crisis equal in intensity to divorce plus redundancy. All the signposts of bereavement are there but the grief is 'unfocused'—no named person to mourn, no body and no ceremony.

Because of the lack of preparation described above and because of pressures against ill-timed conception, the diagnosis of infertility usually comes as a shock. It is a loss all the more hard to bear because it goes unacknowledged by the world in general, and because of the degree of secrecy involved. Couples don't wish to proclaim the 'failure' of their most intimate moments, thus shutting out their ordinary support systems. Friends and family are still waiting for the great announcement —all the more reason for the counsellor to acknowledge and comprehend the magnitude of their pain.

The Medical Scene—

Investigation, treatment, outcome

It is impossible for a lay person to keep abreast of development in the 'treatment' of infertility, for these change almost daily. Drugs, micro-surgery and assisted conception techniques all vary in availability both geographically and between the public and private sectors.

General handbooks in the bookshops may be of some value in preparing patients for standard investigations and in listing the treatments for different conditions. However when it comes to detail they are out of date almost as soon as they are published. Most clinics produce their own leaflets/handbooks describing treatments on offer and what they entail for the patient. These have the advantage of being regularly updated. If you are supporting a client through investigation or treatment, it helps to get a copy of the clinic's handbook.

Since the arrival in 1978 of the first 'Test Tube Baby' and the media emphasis on 'miracles', it is no surprise that individuals have their hopes quite improperly raised. It is difficult for them to sort out where to begin. Within the NHS there are long waiting lists for assisted conception with geographical variations in availability and selection criteria.

In the many private clinics, treatment costs run quickly to four figures and clinics vary in whom they are willing to take on. Moreover, some centres for their own excellent reasons insist on starting again at the beginning with initial investigations, and the thought of 'going through all that again' may deter couples from shopping around.

Sadly, the opposite also applies—there are desperate individuals who move from one clinic to another, fruitlessly, unrealistically hoping for a baby. A period of 10 years' investigations and treatment is not uncommon. I know one couple who persevered for 14 years, the quest for that unreachable child becoming a way of life.

It is difficult for them, and for us, to comprehend statistics for 'success'. For the patient, 'success' means a baby in their arms; it may mean something slightly different to the doctors. One of the roles of the counsellor at every stage must be to encourage those undergoing treatment to look realistically at current success rates. They are still small.

Although clinics are required to publish success rates, these throw no light on the management of patients and their circumstances. For example, one clinic with apparently promising take-home-baby percentages may be depending heavily on Donor Insemination. Another may look more seriously at consequences for parents and the resulting child.

The Human Fertilisation &
Embryology Act 1990

Private clinics providing infertility treatment are licensed by the Human Fertilisation & Embryology Authority (HFEA), as a result of recommendations made in the Warnock Report (1984). In addition to regulating medical and scientific practice, the Act concerns itself with matters of social policy related to patients undergoing treatment, the children born as a result and donors of gametes.

Clinics are subject to annual inspection, being licensed to carry out a limited range of procedures within tight guidelines. The HFEA Code of Practice is updated regularly and gives detailed guidance on counselling requirements. It can be obtained from the HFEA - address at the back of this book.

The Code of Practice gives guidance on all aspects of the work of in vitro fertilisation, donor insemination, research centres, staff, premises, equipment, assessment of patients and donors, the welfare of the child, information to be given to patients and donors, the storage and handling of gametes and embryos, consent, counselling, security and complaints.

It requires that people seeking licensed treatment or consenting to the use or storage of embryos, donation or storage of gametes, must be given 'a suitable opportunity to receive proper counselling about the implications of taking the proposed steps'. While it is mandatory for clinics and centres to offer counselling, the client's acceptance of counselling is voluntary; surveys suggest that particularly in the private sector the offer is not taken up. The HFEA identifies three areas for which counselling should be available: implications of treatment, support and therapy.

Many private clinics are quite compact, staffed for instance by a Director, consultant gynaecologist, nurse, counsellor and secretary, with other specialist resources brought in as required. It would appear that some clinics are not necessarily applying the HFEA's criteria for counsellors: Chartered Psychologist, CQSW or BAC Accredited. The HFEA are currently looking at the training levels of counsellors and providing guidance to clinics. BAC members are involved in this process.

It is the HFEA's requirement that the counsellor be 'independent' and not part of 'assessment' which is particularly difficult for somebody operating as a member of a small team. From the client's point of view, if the counsellor works within the clinic there is always the suspicion that s/he has an assessment function and might recommend treatment being discontinued—enough to render the client cautious about seeking help with emotional difficulties.

For some clinics the 'independence' clause is the go-ahead to refer to an outside counsellor, but if a clinic team have limited perceptions of a counsellor's role they may operate varying criteria for making a referral. The situation is clouded further when this means extra expense for the client. There must be some whose need for counselling goes unrecognised. Clinic personnel may genuinely believe a brief discussion of treatment implications is enough.

However, there are positives: where qualified counsellors are employed and particularly within the larger NHS hospitals offering a range of investigations and treatment, standards are high. In 1988 the British Infertility Counselling Association (BICA) was set up to promote just such a service. A national body, with local and regional networks, BICA provides valuable informal meetings, as well as more structured seminars. It publishes a quarterly newsletter and is a member of BAC espousing its Codes of Ethics & Practice.

Basic information, causes of
infertility and current procedures

... the first flutter of a baby felt in the womb,
Its little signal and promise of riches to come,
Is taken in its father's name ....
from *For a Child Expected* by **Ann Ridler**

In this chapter I am including only enough general information for counsellors to appreciate the implications of the various causes of infertility and the procedures involved. Methods of diagnosis, procedures and solutions are changing at such a rate it would be wrong to attempt more; they also vary geographically and between specific clinics.

If you need fuller details and can handle medical texts, take qualified advice on what to read. The booklist includes handbooks designed for the general public—do ensure you get the most up to date edition.

For regularly updated, brief, informative leaflets on the main causes and treatments, refer to Issue (formerly National Association for the Childless) address, page 51. If you have a client who is receiving treatment, the hospital or clinic may provide a patients' handbook which would help you, too.

Fertility testing

The GP
The decision to seek medical advice is a watershed - see Chapter 5. It is the GP who makes the referral to a specialist, so most enquiries start at the local practice. GPs vary considerably in their approach, understanding and interest in this field. For some couples it is undoubtedly their GP's personal support that keeps them going through the years of treatment. Others take the line 'You don't die of infertility, and there are enough children in the world anyway'.

Of course it may be right for a couple who have only had a few months unprotected intercourse to be advised to 'go away and keep on trying', 'relax, have a holiday', 'forget about it', or a combination of these accompanied by brief information about human fertility time-scales. But if their anxiety is high, they find this rejecting.

Where a couple have been trying for some time, if either partner is over 30 or there is something relevant in their medical histories, the GP will probably instigate investigations immediately.

The GP should go fully into both health backgrounds, lifestyle factors (including work environment), contraception methods, any pregnancies and should check whether full intercourse is taking place and how often. (A small percentage may have problems of sexual technique, where psycho-sexual counselling is indicated.) There should be a physical examination to eliminate obvious abnormality. The GP may recommend a healthier lifestyle, as tobacco, alcohol, diet and exercise can all affect fertility.

GPs vary in the amount of investigations they perform locally and at what point they refer enquirers to a specialist.

Some GPs may advise counselling at this stage, because of concerns about aspects of the relationship, sex life or life history.

The Clinic
Most patients are referred to a gynaecologist. There are some 1,000 gynaecology consultants in the UK; infertility represents a small proportion of their work. Couples may have to attend outpatients alongside antenatal patients and women seeking termination of pregnancy. It is still quite common for an appointment to be offered only to the woman, with the request that she bring along a specimen of semen from her partner.

The range of tests (depending on previous medical history) might include:

Cervical Mucus Test — swab to ensure mucus is normal.
Endometrial Biopsy — done under local anaesthetic, the lining of the womb is examined to ensure ovulation is occurring.
Hormonal Assay — to check hormone levels; a blood sample is taken.
Hysterosalpingogram — a specialised x-ray to check fallopian tubes and the internal structure of the uterus. Involves injection of dye and can be painful.
Laparoscopy — a more complex examination to explore pelvic area usually requiring hospitalisation and general anaesthetic.
Temperature Chart - the woman's temperature has to be taken every morning to determine whether ovulation is occurring.

Tubal Insufflation — to check if fallopian tubes are open. Carbon dioxide is blown into the uterus and the pressure recorded on a graph.

Semen Analysis or Sperm Count — the essential basic test of male fertility. Lab checks include: number of sperm, their ability to move, structure, the volume of the ejaculate. This test must be repeated as levels fluctuate considerably. It is virtually impossible to set arbitrary limits by which a man's fertility can be measured.

Post-Coital Test — to ascertain interaction between the sperm and the female genital tract. The couple have intercourse at ovulation about 12 hours before the test; secretions are examined to see if sperm are surviving within the woman's body and if conception appears possible.

Sperm Invasion Test — to evaluate the possibility of hostile mucus.

This preliminary list may give some idea of clients' experiences. Even where partners want a joint appointment, the investigation usually starts with the woman. From a medical perspective these are routine procedures, but individuals can find them an ordeal; invasive for the woman, with the man feeling left out in the cold. An apparently minor routine such as the daily temperature chart may create enormous pressure, acting as a regular reminder of the problem.

At some stage in these procedures the cause of the infertility may be diagnosed but patients may be offered further appointments without explanation. Even allowing for the recipients' very heightened sensitivities, there's no doubt that the diagnosis is not always sensitively conveyed.

When we remember that these consultations often take place in general gynaecology/antenatal departments, with heavily pregnant women streaming past and photographs of babies on the walls, we can imagine the impact. It is not unusual for clients to report that they were half-way to the car, or back at home, before the implications of what the consultant said sank in.

Not surprisingly this experience sometimes has a knock-on effect on the counselling relationship. Your client might put you in the role of 'expert' who has detailed knowledge of medical procedures; and not knowing where to start may 'rattle off' a list of medical terms to put you in the picture.

So what matters here is to understand what the experience means for the client, perhaps by asking them to describe the procedures and their purpose. This may redress the balance of power. A discussion of the emotional and psychological effects of this sort of medical intervention appears in chapter 5.

I must emphasise that infertility investigations and treatment constitute a positive experience for many patients, because they feel that at last something is being done. It is inevitable that the counsellor hears more about the bad experiences, and people for whom the outcome has been disappointing are more likely to seek counselling. But there is also evidence that whatever the quality of medical input, a couple's psychological and physical well-being is damaged by protracted clinical investigations.

Causes of Infertility

Again it is sensible to refer counsellors to current handbooks or medical texts to appreciate the finer details of the many causes and manifestations of infertility. A combination of factors in both partners frequently complicates changes of success. Success rates and availability of treatment are changing all the time.

Female Infertility:

Endometriosis
A condition where the lining of the womb spreads outside the womb to cover adjacent organs. Surgery is sometimes required to remove areas of disease and adhesions.

Tubal damage
The fallopian tubes are delicate, about the size of a pencil and can become obstructed following infection or after abdominal surgery.

Ovulatory disorders
A spectrum of problems which includes complete absence of menstruation. These conditions are normally treated by medication.

Congenital defects
These can include absence or malformation of all or some reproductive organs.

Ectopic pregnancy
Pregnancy which occurs outside the uterus, usually calling for crisis surgery, often leads to tubal damage.

Miscarriage and stillbirth
As many as one in five pregnancies end in a miscarriage. The problem of habitual miscarriage arises when a woman has suffered three or more consecutive miscarriages—there are a wide range of causes.

Sterilisation
This can be reversed, but requires major surgery.

Secondary infertility
Infertility following the birth of one child—cause can be most of those listed above.

Age
A very important factor for women; female fertility reduces gradually from 30 onwards, more rapidly after 35. This is an increasing problem as many women defer the decision about child-bearing for relationship and career reasons.

Male Infertility
Most people know little about the male reproductive system. In schools it is the female system which gets explained in detail. Men are themselves often ignorant about how the system works. Male infertility has traditionally generated less research.

Sperm defects
These include no sperm, low sperm count, poor mobility, abnormal structure.

Varicocele
A type of varicose vein of the testes — can respond to surgery.

Previous Vasectomy
Can be reversed, but assuming no other factors, chances of successful pregnancy are only about 50%.

Congenital defects
Absence or malformation of the reproductive organs.

Joint problems
There is often a combination of factors in both male and female.

Unexplained infertility
About 10% of infertile couples continue infertile without diagnosed cause. Medical opinions vary on the importance of stress and psychological factors. Psychosexual problems undoubtedly cause a small

proportion of these cases, as of course do physical problems which escape current diagnostic methods.

Medical advice
Couples may be advised against having children because of: hereditary risks for the child, risks to the mother, social/medical problems (e.g. disabled parent(s).

Treatments and procedures

Assisted Conception Techniques
Although often described as 'treatments' these techniques do not 'cure' the infertility; they bypass the problem and offer a solution. They demand a high degree of commitment—in terms of physical invasion, complex and intensive drug regimes, time and energy (money too, as they are rarely available on the NHS, though this varies geographically).

Success rates vary but percentages are low. The most common forms are Gametes Intra Fallopian Transfer (GIFT) and In Vitro Fertilisation (IVF)—the original 'test tube baby' procedure. There are other versions; the field is changing as you read this.

Donor Insemination
Useful where there are sperm problems, or hereditary risks on the male side. A relatively simple procedure, but with complex implications discussed elsewhere. Sometimes available on the NHS.

If your client is undergoing assisted conception treatment currently, get a copy of the leaflet provided by their hospital or clinic for an up-to-the-minute detailed picture.

Drugs
There is a wide range of hormonal treatments, regularly modified and updated. Side effects from medication can be lengthy and distressing but do not affect all users alike.

Tubal Surgery
Major abdominal surgery to repair damaged fallopian tubes. Success rates not high but depend on site of the damage.

Surrogacy
The process where one woman bears a child on behalf of another is, of course, not a 'treatment' but it is an option which a small but

significant number of individuals and couples are taking each year and the practice is growing. There are always many more couples wishing to avail themselves of this than there are women offering to act as surrogate mothers.

There are two forms of surrogacy: 'straight', where the surrogate mother will impregnate herself with the commissioning husband's sperm, so the child is genetically hers and the commissioning husband's; 'host', where the surrogate mother is implanted with fertilised embryos donated by the commissioning couple, thereby acting as an 'incubator' for a child that is genetically not hers.

COTS (Childlessness Overcome Through Surrogacy) and its sister organisation Triangle promote the practice by providing the equivalent of a 'dating agency' enabling couples and potential surrogates to meet; it offers support to those undergoing the process. Details are at the back of this book.

There are legal and psychological issues which I have discussed in Chapter 4.

Principles of good practice in
working with infertile clients

Our baby was to be the living sign of our joy,
Restore to each the other's lost infancy ....
from For a Child Expected by Ann Ridler

The Counsellor
Counselling begins with the self and self-knowledge: vital in an area
which touches us all. Perhaps the fertility problem brought the client to
your doorstep or maybe this is one factor among many. Either way, you
are working with a thwarted basic longing and all the grief, rage,
disbelief and disappointment brought about by a denial of this 'right'.

Feelings
Sometimes the strength of one's own feelings can take the counsellor
by surprise. It's important for the work ahead to explore these feelings
honestly, even if some of them are unpalatable. Regular supervision is
the best setting for this. Working with infertility has something in
common with bereavement counselling and an occasional weariness is
common to both. It is a natural reaction and a healthy reminder of how
the client must be feeling.

I believe that if we honestly acknowledge our own values, beliefs and
feelings we can work with situations and clients towards whom we
might not feel personally drawn, for we still share the task of empowering them to move forward.

It may be the first time you have considered exploring your own feelings
about childlessness and putting them into words. For instance, do you
have a positive picture of a childfree lifestyle? If you were pressed,
would you reply 'Life without children is not worth living'? On the other
hand, your first uncensored thought might be that childfree means
carefree but selfish and materialistic.

There are moral issues too that may touch a chord. What do you feel about

- the cost of infertility treatment (in time and money)? After all the infertile are not ill?
- the intense pursuit of treatment over years?
- assisted conception techniques and the demands on patients where success rates are low?
- donor insemination, the feelings of the donor, the rights of the child to know about its origins?
- the usage of stored embryos or sperm?
- termination of pregnancy and the rights of the unborn child? A client who felt pressurised into having a termination as a teenager may be sitting before you now in her mid-thirties, distraught at being unable to conceive again. She may see her present infertility as a 'punishment' for the abortion.
- individuals who have been sterilised and seek reversal later?
- single, rather than infertile, applicants seeking treatment, e.g. those planning to remain a single parent or in a lesbian relationship? One partner may have undergone a sex change.
- disabled people who hope to conceive against medical advice?
- people in their 40s who are 'still trying'?
- women with a partner over 60 who will be an old man before the child grows up?

Fortunately you only need to explore the points which apply to current work. The ongoing exploration with a supervisor will keep pace with your work with the client. This work is vitalising and endlessly new because it encompasses this basic area of human experience.

Children's Needs

Feelings run deep on what children need and what constitutes 'good enough' parenting. So how do you perceive your clients as potential parents? It is important for counsellors to realise that they aren't looking for parents for themselves. Your subconscious may flag up: 'I wouldn't want those two for my mum and dad'—fortunately that is not the scenario. Perhaps you are worried that the client sitting before you wants a child so desperately that no living baby could fill the bill.

Besides offering support, the counsellor shares the client's task of looking at current and future choices and helping them move towards healing and acceptance at their pace. How possible then is it to work with clients whose parenting ability is open to question?

Perhaps you know of domestic violence, instability, serious mental health problems, other life history factors not shared with medical staff. Your client perhaps believes the problem will be solved if a child arrives. We do have some responsibility towards any child born following infertility treatment.

However, unless you have a remit to assess would-be recipients of treatment you are not responsible for the decision whether or not to proceed. Nevertheless the calm and honest way you voice your concerns may have more effect than you imagine. Some clients ask for counselling because at one level they need permission to say 'parenting is not for me'.

If you have very serious doubts indeed, based on known facts, you may have to share these with your client. If you are so troubled that you believe you should communicate with the clinic, you should inform your client, unless that puts either of you at risk. Supervision is crucial here alongside reference to BAC Codes of Ethics & Practice on confidentiality.

Empowerment

The previous paragraph deals with the exceptional. In fact a high proportion of infertile people remain childless and working towards acceptance of this reality is one of the goals of counselling, even as we support their progress through treatment.

Any client thrust into the dependent role of patient may feel 'taken over' and powerless. They may decide to put on a brave face at the clinic, doing exactly what they're told for fear of treatment being withdrawn. This makes it harder than ever for them to keep success rates in proportion— for they have to go on hoping.

It can be difficult for patients in this situation to say they need a rest or ask for medical explanations to be repeated. Perhaps they are enduring the uncomfortable side-effects of the drug programme in silence. It is not uncommon for a client entering counselling at this stage to ask wistfully '... do you think counselling will do me good?'

So the counsellor mustn't join the ranks of 'experts' telling the client what to do, even when the client wants to put them there. Paradoxically it is only possible to help someone reclaim their decision-making skills when we have first encouraged them to express their sadness and negativity. This can be taken further, by looking at the success rates of their particular programme and asking them to consider how long they wish to continue treatment. Taking things further still, to encourage them to keep at the back of their mind the positive attributes of a childfree lifestyle.

If the client has got into a tangle in their communication with medical staff, seeing themselves on a conveyor belt, unable to ask questions or express doubt, assertiveness techniques might help. But is an element of magic thinking or fear of 'retribution' getting in the way of their adult relationship with the people geared to help them? If there is, it needs bringing out into the open.

Overspill

If you are working with a client at diagnosis stage, you are both into crisis work. One effect of crisis is the way it takes over every aspect of the victim's life, forcing everything else onto 'hold'. If you knew your client before this point, other work may still temporarily take a back seat—along with your client's ideas on employment, housing, holidays and friendships.

As a result of this, you may need to re-examine any contract previously agreed. But your support is absolutely vital in enabling the client not to get swamped, making clear choice to defer other work only if this is right.

Onward Referral

The existence of licensed clinics and the development of counselling based on the experiences of clients and counsellors working in this specialist field, means that referral on, or asking for consultancy, is possible and should be considered seriously if you feel you are getting stuck.

Issues for the Counsellor

... but the birth of a child is an uncontrollable glory:
Cat's cradle of hopes will hold no living baby,
Long though it lay quietly ...

from *For a Child Expected* by **Ann Ridler**

Content

It's important to get the right balance of support, therapy and implications work. The client's need and your own setting will contribute to this. If your client is undergoing treatment, it's essential to check whether counselling is provided at the clinic. Some clinics employ qualified counsellors, experts in this field who see patients regularly; in this case an overlap of roles won't help.

But there are many places where counselling is limited to an information session with medical staff providing (as required by the HFE Act) exact details of procedures, possible outcomes and likely side-effects. The HFEA Code of Practice emphasises that counselling should be clearly distinguished from information-giving, normal doctor-patient relationship and assessment.

Implications—enabling the client to weigh the pros and cons of treatment but also to consider the effects of *not* going further down that road. It is easy to feel sucked into a 'system' which is difficult to question. Of course your client wants a child—that's what all the investigations were about. But with the next steps looming, suddenly there's no room for ambivalence. Perhaps one partner is eager to press forward, the other less certain. It may be easier to verbalise doubts in the reassuring presence of a counsellor than alone with a partner—if the pain is too raw or emotions too volatile.

Other courses of action may get neglected because of pressure to take the 'logical' step forward. A couple feeling storm-damaged by the investigations may long for a breather while they attend to other aspects of their lives. Even though they have reached the point of being offered treatment they may have mixed feelings and would welcome the chance of looking at a childfree lifestyle or considering other ways of parenting (adoption, surrogacy). They may need help to verbalise this—it seems almost heresy after all they've gone through.

They may need time for grieving or dealing with other emotional work that got elbowed out earlier.

On the other hand, if it feels right to proceed the client needs to look at the short and long term effects of the recommended treatment programme. A demanding programme like IVF with its intensive medication and detailed time-table can affect employment (whether to carry on, take leave, the level of disclosure at work).

Partners may have different perceptions regarding a bearable time-scale for such an all-absorbing series of procedures. Are they prepared for the switchback of hope and disappointment which continues month after month? It is not at all uncommon for one partner to assume the other shares their internal time-scale. If they are attending a private clinic finance is a key issue.

Weighing the pros and cons of surgery or medication may have different implications for either partner. If the infertility is secondary the effect on child(ren) already in the family may need exploring.

What about donor insemination? Have they thought through the implications of informing the child about its origins or of adopting the strict secrecy still recommended by many clinics. What does each partner feel, think and imagine about the donor, the mysterious life-long third party in this arrangement? How will the man feel, knowing that he is not that natural father? What does the woman feel about having another man's seed in her body.

Is he blocking his feelings to give his partner the chance of being a mother? Is she blocking her fantasies because it feels like infidelity? Couples may wish to examine the demands on their own relationship as well as their relationship with others.

Whatever the medical options, the counsellor will help users keep an eye on current success rates—there must be some ongoing preparation for disappointment at every stage and the counsellor's acknowledgement of this may keep the client in touch with reality.

But perhaps this stage is past; your client is doing griefwork and moving towards some kind of acceptance of childlessness. In looking at the implications for their future together, either partner may need help to express their pain to the other—a painful time for the counsellor as well. As in bereavement, individuals require different time-scales for looking at practical and emotional issues and being able to move forward.

Support

As over the months strenuous treatments continue without apparent success, or as couples struggle to come to terms with childlessness but don't 'feel any better', all we can give is support and acceptance.

Families and friends who may have been good listeners at the beginning get tired of hearing 'no change', and re-immerse in their own lives. The situation may be difficult for them too and they want a rest. It is then that the counsellor's support matters most. She may be the only person left who can stay 'where the client is'. The monthly 'switchback' takes an enormous toll of relationships and energy. Active listening, concern and feedback are of more value than we sometimes admit.

Although support can involve sometimes reserving judgement, we should never go along with assumptions that 'everything is going to work out well', nor should the counsellor fail to question or challenge when needed. One aspect of support too is the quiet reassurance that the complex and bewildering range of thoughts and emotions that are going on inside the client are a perfectly normal reaction to the circumstances.

Therapeutic Work

Although infertility can have the effect of swamping other issues, the opposite also applies: grief or shock may unmask other, older pain, providing the opportunity to look at it in a new light. One response to the question 'Why now, why me?' may be for the client to look again at childhood, previous relationships, past sexual behaviour, old losses, or even fantasies which the client links with the present problem.

Perhaps the need for therapeutic work lies in the infertility itself — a man no longer feels virile, a woman 'failed her own parents'. For some the fact of bringing out these feelings and having them acknowledged is itself therapeutic.

But the work is elastic and the counsellor may be in a position to open up matters relating to: finance, employment, social relationships, cultural specific issues, partnership and sexuality, or inter-personal reactions: depression, anxiety, confidence and self-esteem. The individual's own experience of being parented, or early significant relationships and any indirect experience of infertility are all relevant.

Who is suitable for treatment?

There is considerable variation in the criteria clinics adopt. As well as medical considerations some clinics apply age-limits, some take married people only. Others do consider the single or gay (who may not be biologically infertile). A few offer treatment to women who have passed the menopause (again, not technically infertile).

The HFEA Code of Practice places on clinics a clear responsibility to consider the welfare of the child: 'a woman shall not be provided with treatment services unless account has been taken of the welfare of any child who may be born as a result of the treatment—including the need of that child for a father—and of any other child who may be affected by the birth'. This means that some centres will not take on lesbian couples or single women.

Centres are required to take reasonable steps to ascertain who would be the legal parents (or parent) and who it is intended will be bringing him or her up. They are asked to bear in mind the commitment to parenthood of the woman and any partner.

Screening varies: some clinics will veto on grounds of emotional unsuitability, others will give this only nominal attention. Similarly, the amount of attention given to attitudes towards the child, to family circumstances and the views of the extended family, varies from one clinic to another.

Whatever the grounds for treatment being refused, some unhappy couples despairingly do the rounds. Maybe they have 'not heard' medical or other advice, maybe they have had a raw deal. It is not unknown for individuals to pursue a succession of treatment options for 12-15 years in a distressed and obsessional manner. By offering a different quality of attention it may be the counsellor's role to get them to look afresh at this tortured pilgrimage and ask themselves if the time has come to call a halt, or to deal with the disappointment that clinics' criteria for selection pose for them.

There are times too when the counsellor feels torn between the requirements of doctors, patients, society and the law. Perhaps s/he possesses a fuller picture of the client than the clinic. So where does the counsellor stand who knows:
- of Schedule 1 offences in the client's history which suggest a child might be at risk within this family, or

- that children of either partner have been removed or are in care, or
- of health factors, mental or physical, which suggest the client would be put at serious risk by pregnancy or parenting?
It is here that private ethical concerns impinge on the public domain. The counsellor should apply BAC Code of Ethics & Practice, section B.4 and B.5 with intensive supervision and guidance.

Enabling the client to retain/regain control

Ambivalence about parenthood is a normal, understandable reaction to a gigantic life change. People grieving because they are childless lose sight of these ordinary mixed feelings. It is even harder to voice them in the presence of partners, family, friends, clinic personnel, and while treatment is going on. But blocking out these mixed feelings is poor preparation for parenthood, because it implies that a child will result in perfect happiness.

Taking this further, people need the opportunity to voice honest doubts about how far to pursue their quest. It is an important part of the counsellor's job to listen 'between the words' for self-questioning or mixed feelings. By honouring these healthy reactions, the client regains more choice and power of decision. It is particularly difficult when two partners move at different paces. This calls for sharing and negotiation in a safe setting. After all, it is everybody's right to say "We must keep going", or "No more", but they may need support in dealing with the consequences of this.

Working with one partner only

Women seek counselling more often than men; the typical client is a woman on her own, giving the counsellor a one-eyed view. The woman may have already adopted the 'sick' role, having been 'sent along' by her partner. The counsellor mustn't collude with this viewpoint for the client has acted responsibly in making this choice. It could be tempting to fall into the opposite trap, allocating the sick role to the absent partner, an easy target.

The childishness of the childless

This characteristic is a particularly trying element and very testing to the patience and acceptance of the counsellor. For crisis often brings regression. In this scenario, one spouse sinks gracelessly into childishness, almost begging their partner to act as Mum or Dad. When this behaviour also meets a temporary need in partner number two, the result can be a tragic folie a deux: sulking, tantrums, over-dependency, comfort-seeking, trouble over daily decisions... or it may run into obsession with pets, collectibles, toys, the paraphernalia of Mothercare, games, equipment and fantasies about a non-existent baby.

Naturally the client wants to involve the counsellor in this flight from reality. It calls for a demanding mix of clarity and tenderness, plus persistent raising of the client's awareness about what is happening. Feeling more in charge of their own lives and moving together towards joint decision-making is a way of counteracting this phase, which is damaging only if people get stuck.

Factors relating to different medical

situations

There is a good deal of overlap between being infertile and being childless but different causes carry specific reactions, so it's important that the counsellor remembers 'where it all began'.

Miscarriage/ectopic pregnancy

"Well, at least we know I can get pregnant", the client declares, but such knowledge leaves a bitter taste. The event itself may have been a traumatic medical emergency, accompanied, in the case of ectopic pregnancy, by searing physical pain. It's quite likely there was no aftercare whatsoever. Not surprisingly the sufferer needs to re-live the trauma again and again apparently without relief.

Because the event constituted a medical emergency, the client may have been treated insensitively, ending up in a maternity ward surrounded by mothers and babies. The couple might have been told about the loss in an inappropriate way. The woman could have been discharged from hospital once the crisis was over without a chance to talk things over.

There may not have been an opportunity to grieve the lost infant. Counsellors working with stillbirth and miscarriage report that mementos, photographs, finger or foot prints and rites of passage play a big part in healing. Even so, the invisible anniversaries, of the trauma and of the time when the child would have been born, bring up the pain again.

Moreover this non-existent child can form a 'safe' subject for quite relentless parental fantasy; for instance parents become convinced it would have excelled in some way.

Guilt comes in—the client 'knows' something she did or felt brought about the disaster. "I didn't want this baby to start with" ... "I didn't love my partner enough" ... "I shouldn't have continued swimming/working/ decorating" ... etc. These run alongside a kind of hopeful despair. "At least I can get pregnant", while a further pregnancy is accompanied, understandably, by intense anxiety.

Was it a real pregnancy (i.e. with biochemical and ultrasonic evidence, a clinical diagnosis)? There are times when the account of a 'miscarriage' has an unreal quality, no medical opinion but perhaps a positive result from a test from the chemists, followed eventually by menstruation and heart-break. Here the counsellor, unsure of the facts, sits uncomfortably at the crossroads between inner and outer reality. I believe the counsellor has to stay with the woman's miscarriage experience for the time being.

Previous termination/sterilisation
Past decisions, apparent solutions, bring present remorse. The client 'knows' the termination brought about the infertility. But the client made what was 'the best decision' at the time and needs support in recognising this. It is easy to get stuck in self-blame. Alternatively, possibly they blame somebody else: parents, partner, doctor and this needs exploring.

Male Infertility
Infertility is still traditionally the province of the female, so the discovery of a male problem can come like a bolt from the blue. And here it's harder for a man to express his feelings at being labelled 'impotent and less of a man'—as he sees it. He's less likely to risk disclosure to friends/ colleagues/family, fearing ribaldry ("the lad's got no lead in his pencil") or incomprehension. Parents can be dumbfounded, quickly disowning blame: "We can't have done anything wrong, he was always a fit and lively boy". So men are thrown more upon their inner resources.

Some men aren't too clear why they want fatherhood, so their painful feelings are vague and inexpressible. There is a strong pressure to 'carry on regardless'—immerse themselves in work. But for the person who sees himself as the 'cause', his partner's grief is hard to bear. Guilt blocks his ability to offer comfort.

Unexplained infertility

This takes its own particular toll. The couple have done their best by having all the tests done but things are no clearer than before. They may launch into an endless search for a second opinion; each may fantasise that 'things might have been better with X...' (alternative partner). The lack of diagnosis is compounded by pressures from well-wishers: "It's just a question of learning to relax", or "Isn't there somebody else you can see?"

There is an element of reality in some of this. 'Unexplained' can mean 'under-investigated'. There is always anecdotal evidence of couples who 'went through everything' with one clinic, only to get a fuller diagnosis and better results elsewhere. This adds to the anxiety.

Donor Insemination

This is one solution to male infertility. It involves the short-term demands of a carefully timed treatment programme with its intense switchback of hope and disappointment. More seriously there are life-long implications for parents and child: living with the 'difference' and dealing with the knock-on effects this has on their relationship and the relationship with others. Do they opt for secrecy and learn to live with a time-bomb? Do they search for ways of informing their nearest and dearest, and eventually the child, about its origins?

Clients on donor insemination programmes need support to stay in the world of reality and each partner has their own needs. They may have fantasies they cannot share about the donor. They need to understand the practical issues involved in selection and screening. If they've decided not to tell anybody the exact nature of the treatment this can set up a private ordeal for the male partner who may feel marginalised as well as being the 'cause' of what the woman's going through. He may have consented initially for his partner's sake but developed strong resistance later. If a baby comes along, he has to put on a brave face and join in the 'whoopees' all round.

He really does need encouragement to put his feelings into words in complete safety—this is an excellent time to see partners separately.

In-Vitro Fertilisation (or similar)

The main factor for the woman is the immersing nature of the treatment, the powerful medication and split second timing of each procedure, plus the uncertainty. She may have to 'act as normal' with friends and at work, still not daring to raise her hopes. Besides being physically exhausted she may feel taken over and need support in remaining her own person.

If she gets pregnant there's a higher-than-normal likelihood of multiple birth; she may have to decide if some embryos should be 'culled' to improve chances.

At a deeper level, assisted conception techniques replace the ordinary sexual union with an 'immaculate conception', which must affect the relationship. The flow is broken from intimacy to conception and childbirth, and the link between the mother's body and her eggs is lost. Parents who have had a child by this method still speak of the loss of this normal process.

Medication
It's worth bearing in mind that drugs prescribed to boost ovulation can have powerful side effects, physical and emotional. Depression and loss of libido are not uncommon, escalating as treatment continues. Again clients may need support in recognising their right to call a halt if they wish. The very fact that they can unload the burden and that the counsellor doesn't urge them to 'carry on at all costs' may make it easier to count the cost of keeping going and how long it's acceptable to do so.

Congenital defects
Some people choose childlessness on medical advice for fear of passing on a hereditary condition or on the grounds that they are themselves unable to cope with childbearing/parenting. Their sense of loss parallels the experience of clients grappling with infertility. The face that they have 'always known' makes no difference.

This sense of loss is highlighted at points of transition throughout life. Anybody working with the elderly or terminally ill will know that a man or woman needs time and support to reflect on what it has meant not to have children and to acknowledge their sadness if it is still there.

Men and women born without all or some of their reproductive organs can feel peculiarly set apart. There are possibly endochrinological and chromosomal irregularities calling for lifelong hormonal treatment as well as plastic surgery. While they share the problems of the childless, their situation is compounded by their wish for secrecy. Indeed ongoing reserve may become a way of life, putting a permanent veto on close relationships.

It is particularly likely that information about their condition was communicated clumsily and that their parents had no help in handling the situation. It is not so long ago that a woman would be refused reconstructive vaginal surgery unless she could produce a fiancé and demonstrate bona fide marriage plans!

Since these conditions are relatively rare, isolation is inevitable, although there is now some move towards openness particularly among younger women. Support networks are getting going. But it is still a lonely path to tread. The bitterness of the blow, the isolation and the effect on key relationships colour everything.

Surrogacy

For a woman giving eggs or embryos, or acting as surrogate a programme very similar to IVF may be involved. I've described the difference between 'straight' and 'host' surrogacy but to my mind the implications vary even more greatly depending on whether the surrogate is a 'stranger' (introduced by an agency) or whether she is a relative or friend of the 'commissioning parents'.

Either way, the dynamics of the relationship between all parties and the child carry a lifelong emotional charge which can be extremely complex. The complexity is increased further in within-family surrogacy if secrecy is involved and information about its origins are withheld from the child. In these circumstances an emotional 'time-bomb' exists within the family circle, very similar to that created by an in-family adoption.

An important role for the counsellor (who may well have strong feelings about the situation which need working through in supervision) is to encourage all parties involved to think through the implications both for themselves and for other members of the family, especially other children who may be related to the child borne by the surrogate mother.

a)   Some issues for the commissioning couple:
Is this something they both want equally?
Trust: will be would-be surrogate stick to the agreement?

Control: can they insist on:
1) the surrogate mother taking 'adequate' care during pregnancy (including not smoking, for instance);
2) on additional tests (e.g. amniocentesis) if there are medical concerns;
3) termination   in   the   case   of   possible   disability,
4) the surrogate's willingness to carry a multiple conception to term;
5) a further attempt if there is a miscarriage. Couples may feel they would like to 'own' the surrogate during the pregnancy, with knowledge and control over her every move.

Contact: (in the case of a 'stranger' surrogacy) throughout the pregnancy; face to face; telephone only? Who is to be present at the birth? Ongoing contact with the child as life goes on?

b)   Issues for the surrogate mother:
Motivation: have her own needs to parent been met; is her family complete; if she is a relative or friend of the couple, is she impelled to help them out of guilt or pity and unaware of the lifelong implications for them all? Is there family pressure? If she is a stranger is the motivation financial? Is having a baby the only thing at which she believes herself to be good?

Her confidence in the couple to be 'good enough' parents to 'her' child —including the level of confidence in their relationship and physical and mental health. Can she trust them to take the baby as promised. Will they tell the child the truth about its origins? Will they keep to contact agreements?

Her own family situation, views of partner and existing children. What is she planning to tell people if she comes home empty-handed from hospital. Is there practical backup during the pregnancy?

Whatever the motivation, there are lifelong implications for a surrogate mother and her family not unlike losing a child to adoption: bereavement, regret, guilt, loss of contact, a longing for information later on, sometimes an inability to move forward in her own life because of the difficulty of coming to terms with a decision which appeared to be 'for the best' at the time.

Contrary to popular belief, surrogacy is perfectly legal, provided no fee changes hands and reasonable expenses only are paid. The child's birth is registered jointly in the names of the commissioning father and birth mother.

However there is no legal obligation on the surrogate mother to hand over the infant. Honesty and a calm examination of the issues is particularly difficult where an intense emotional climate prevails. There are legal changes on the way aimed at protecting the interests of children caught up in surrogacy agreements that go awry.

Ways of working

Each counsellor has their own model and clients feel comfortable with some variations but not others.

Guided visualisation
One way of helping somebody undergoing treatment to get a sense of responding to it fully. I am assuming you're familiar with the basic techniques of this method. You can either take your client through each phase of the treatment in a very literal fashion, guiding them step by step, emphasising confidence, healing and a successful outcome; or the visualisation can be purely metaphorical following an imaginary journey with a series of obstacles successfully overcome.

Deeper hypnotic methods can be employed to access subconscious blocks to fertility.

Dialogue with 'empty chair'
A technique from Gestalt therapy. Facing an empty chair, the client imagines somebody from their past, present or future, sitting there, with whom there are unresolved issues. Supported by the counsellor the client addresses this key figure. When they reach a natural break or at the counsellor's instigation, the client swaps chairs and speaks as the other. In this way a mother might name and dialogue with a stillborn child, finding a way to say 'goodbye'. A level of insight and acceptance can sometimes be attained in a relatively economical way.

Dreamwork
Dreams sometimes throw a creative searchlight onto daytime dilemmas. An exploration of dream material may get the client 'out of her head' to a more intuitive level—contacting resistances, ambiguities, fears, hopes and fantasies censored by the day-to-day person who has to 'cope' at all costs. There are many dreamwork methods well documented. What matters is that the counsellor resists interpretation and stays tuned to what the dream means to the client.

'Parental messages'
A concept from Transactional Analysis. Get the client to list any messages they may have received in childhood on the subject of childbearing/fertility/parenting. It can be quite fun to start by keeping this light, jotting the messages down at speed without too much reflection: "It's no fun being a mother" or "We've got things to hand down to the next generation". The client can reflect on these in greater depth and explore those with lasting impact (for or against).

Assertiveness techniques
Appropriate when the client is acting, and feeling, the subject of a takeover bid. "I daren't ask the clinic again", "I can't tell my partner I want to change our plan", "I don't want to confront my parents/boss". A simple exploration of the behaviour they wish to change, followed by a role-play practising the chosen new behaviour can be empowering.

Stress Management
Accepting childlessness or going through infertility treatment must parallel divorce, bereavement and moving house in terms of the stress engendered. But because this particular stress is largely 'invisible' socially, clients fail to make any allowance for themselves. Stress comes out in physical symptoms: sleep disturbance, eating patterns, aches and pains, bowel upsets, tiredness or irritability as well as the psychological manifestations we might expect. The counsellor might explore what resources (inner and outer) the client has at their disposal and how they have responded to stress in the past. They may find it helpful to check if there is any part of their life where they could let up a bit.

There is a case for suspecting some infertility to be stress-related; certainly there is anecdotal evidence of those who 'forgot all about it' because of life-change/adoption/holiday/bereavement, only to find that a baby was on the way after all.

Groupwork
I see a place for groupwork which enables people with the same problem to share mutual support. This is not to be confused with the self-help groups clinics put on (for patients going through IVF for instance). A therapeutic group needs to be carefully structured and facilitated by an experienced groupworker. It should probably be single sex and closed group. Only within this framework is it likely to provide a safe environment for full expression of feelings and countering the usual jealousy and competitiveness.

Useful theories for exploration

Bereavement/Grief Model
It is frequently said that working with infertility is very similar to working with bereavement, with the important difference that there is no body to mourn and no anniversary of the loss... Childlessness is not a single event, experiences modify over time, feelings wax and wane in association with other life events.

Reactions to the stress of infertility can follow a pattern akin to bereavement: surprise > denial > isolation > anger > guilt > depression > acceptance/resolution but of course a simple linear process cannot be expected—wave formations or spirals might provide a more suitable metaphor. It is useful to consider the phases described in the literature as a series of signposts.

Individuals can find themselves 'stuck' in one mode, and within a partnership pain and misunderstanding can be intensified if one partner deals with the aspects differently and at a different pace. Many of the symptoms which accompany grief and bereavement can occur, bodily disturbances of all kinds, feelings of emptiness, a preoccupation with images of the 'lost one'—in this case one who has never existed, exaggerated guilt and self-accusation, changes in patterns of activity.

In counselling the bereaved, it is often found necessary to encourage clients to recall in detail the events that led up to the loss, the circumstances surrounding it and experiences following it. For infertile clients, apart from the obvious experiences of diagnosis and treatment, they may need to focus on life events which they see as relevant and go into these in similar detail.

Advice, of course, is out but a necessary step in coping with any stressful situation is the seeking out and utilisation of new information. Supporting and assisting the client in doing this is one of the counsellor's many tasks. Support organisations, relevant literature, alternative treatments, adoption and fostering are obvious areas, but something related to other aspects of the client's life may be just what is needed.

Attachment theory
'A way of conceptualising the propensity of human beings to make strong affectional bonds to particular others and of explaining the anger, anxiety, depression and emotion detachment to which unwilling separation and loss gives rise.' (Bowlby)

Considered in conjunction with the concept of dependency needs or 'object relations' this account of personal development is relevant in all counselling transactions, as borne out by the bulky literature which expands on the subject. It is particularly important when exploring the use made of the client/counsellor relationship and again this is an area to work with in supervision.

When we look at the situation of those facing their own infertility, clients may find their experience with previous attachment figures affects relationships with the clinic (or representative medical personnel) and even the much-longed-for child.

We know that the threat of loss arouses anxiety. Clients may 'cling' to the clinic (conceived of as 'stronger' or 'wiser') when further treatment is really no longer practicable. This may lead to pursuing treatments for an inappropriate length of time, if the attachment has been a positive one.

When the experience has been negative or the trust between patient and medical personnel has been broken, the patient may get caught up in complaints procedures/litigation. Of course it is right to complain where wrong information has been given or mistakes made, but is the client getting 'stuck' in an entanglement that is no longer in their own interests? By understanding the client's previous responses to separation and loss the counsellor may help them see what is happening and perhaps to change their pattern.

It may be that people who have themselves experienced poor parenting, not having their own dependency needs adequately met, can suffer such strong unconscious yearnings for love and a compulsive need to care that their relationship with the longed-for child is already distorted. At some unconscious level lies a belief that a child can resolve all their aching need. These desperate seekers find quite exceptional difficulty in letting go of their hopes of conception and reaching any kind of resolution or acceptance.

The counsellor may be able to help them throw light on this by exploring with them previous departures, illnesses, deaths and arrivals, not to apportion blame but to trace causal chains and to bring some kind of release if possible.

Crisis Theory

Crisis is a term often used to describe the effects of childlessness—it certainly calls into question much that was taken for granted previously. A diagnosis of infertility can constitute a classic crisis which follows the pattern described by Caplan, and other crises may peak over the years, as a result of internal events (such as one partner resolving not to continue with treatment) or 'external' happenings (such as a miscarriage or a failure in treatment).

Much depends on the point at which people seek counselling or if they are already seeing a counsellor. It may be that other personal events have re-awakened the infertility crisis. Only counsellor and client between them can decide whether this is a situation which calls for the very specific intervention skills, or the 'crisis' lies in the reaction rather than the triggering events.

Events might consist of a severe loss of status, possessions or loved ones. The crisis is experienced as a state of serious disorganisation in which the sufferer faces frustration of important life goals or a profound disruption in their life-cycles. Usual coping mechanisms appear ineffective or to have deserted the person altogether.

The following sequence is described:

(a) Initial tension—attempts to deal with it with customary problem solving responses.

(b) Tension mounting, client 'can't think straight', ordinary responses not working; there is frustration, increasing distress, inefficiency in many areas of functioning and failure to adjust.

(c) Peak or acute phase—if not resolved or averted or dealt with internally by denial or resignation there may be major dysfunction in behaviour or loss of self-control.

A 'true' crisis is of short duration and self-limiting. Does your client perceive it as a threat, a loss or a challenge? On the positive side the client can be very receptive to help during a short period and the seeds of considerable growth and change can be stirred into life. A good time for intervention where the outcome can be productive. But it is the case that individuals vary enormously in the resources they have to draw upon. A specific difficulty here is that the crisis is often hidden from others and the couple or individual have to try to maintain their ordinary lives as usual.

Another feature of crisis is that it brings back to the surface other unresolved issues from the past; this can intensify or distort its significance for one partner only, adding to the problems.

If after careful discussion and appraisal a crisis within this limited definition is identified, the client is not in a position to weight the pros and cons of any long-term contract; anything of this nature will have to go on 'hold' in favour of short-term work focused on helping the client return to a reasonable level of functioning. This may include working together on breaking the problem down into manageable segments. It should certainly include an exploration of existing or new support systems.

Life Stages

Erikson constructed a chart showing life unfolding in observable sequences, each stage being marked by a crisis (not a catastrophe but a turning point), psychological development proceeding by critical steps. In describing the three stages of adulthood, each stage is preparatory to that which follows after and has its own essential tasks.

'Intimacy' is the key issue for the early adult (aged 20-30), followed by 'generativity'—becoming a parent—with 'integrity' marking the point of maturity and representing some kind of resolution. Thus parenthood is seen as an essential step on the road to maturity and the development of the capacity for intimacy has been laying the foundation for this.

Adults who miss out on the enrichment of generativity, he warns, will lapse into prolonged stagnation. Often they will begin to indulge themselves as if they were their own child. This links in with the fact that many couples feel or imagine that a principal source of pressure to have children comes from their own parents—who naturally wish to see them acquire full adult status.

The unwilling childless may feel themselves stuck at stage one with all their contemporaries apparently flying past them on the way to the winning post. Even the generation below are beginning to overtake. If the search for the child becomes over-prolonged with no real level of acceptance, they may miss out on the fulfilment that comes with maturity. As counsellors, we can hardly regard parenthood as an essential life stage, desirable though it may be; maturity comes with acceptance as much as with achievement.

For many people the life plan and goals they have constructed for themselves go largely unverbalised. They may have a very full picture of what they want in career terms or the kind of housing they would eventually like, but just imagine large areas of their lives unrolling, as richly patterned as a Turkish carpet, with little help or direction from themselves. It can be useful to encourage clients to draw out a life-map or draw up lists of what they want for themselves in many areas of life — it may be a surprise to everybody and be of considerable value in looking at choices, options and alternatives.

Sociological perspectives

Inability to meet norms, especially those held to be important, is usually equated with failure—deviance can be implied. Even though their deviance is not of their own choosing, infertile people experience adjustment problems in terms of their perception of themselves and perception by significant others.

In fact we might argue that statistically the infertile are 'less deviant' with the increasing trend towards fewer children per family. Not only has the average age of mothers risen on bearing their first child (from 24 years in 1971 to 27.5 in 1991) and no doubt continues to rise, but the average number of dependent children in a family is now 1.8.

A Mintel study of family life styles suggests that nearly 25% of parents with children under 16 say they would have enjoyed freedom from the responsibility of bringing them up. Even the UK Association of the International Year of the Family has not specifically defined what a family is.

Nevertheless the infertile perceive themselves and are perceived as deviant, and a household consisting of two unrelated adults is not usually regarded as a family. The concept of reference group is helpful here. Who do the couple look up to and seek to align themselves with? How realistic are their internalised models—could they, with support, consider alternatives?

Other useful concepts are those of discrepant roles, 'spoilt identity', 'destructive information' and 'dark secrets' propounded by Goffman— 'Facts, known and concealed, which are incompatible with the image that the individual or couple attempt to maintain before their audience'. Even when family and friends are aware of the facts or some of them, the stigma of infertility is not instantly recognisable and the sufferers are from time to time in a state of tension about self-presentation, which then requires special management.

Issues for the Client

"..... all that our passion would yield
We put to planning our child."

from **For a Child Expected** by **Ann Ridler**

Naming the anxiety

You may be working with a couple who have not yet reached this watershed or it may be so distant that they can hardly remember life before they adopted the infertile role. It is a watershed reached by each person in their unique way. Within a partnership differences over the timing of this stage can be a source of great pain or it can be a relief to find the partner is in a similar state of mind. Perhaps one partner only is getting counselling and the experiences of the other partner are reported or implied.

For some people the anguish of childlessness can crystalise for ever at this early stage. Either they deny the problem or a partner refuses to accept it exists and the years go by. A thousand factors past and present converge in this one moment of acknowledging 'something is wrong'.

It's possible that the counselling itself may be the catalyst. The client and counsellor may be working together on another issue.

There are similar variations between partners when it comes to making a decision to look for help—5 minutes or 5 years may elapse before this step is taken. There may be a hundred reasons to put it off, for it entails 'coming out' even if only in a limited way in relation to the medical profession.

Once the problem has been given a name, a strange journey begins. Medical help is elicited and a process set in motion: investigation ... diagnosis. stop: decision ... treatment 1: result. stop: decision ... treatment 2 ... etc. This sets off a quick descent into the patient role, with all the powerlessness this implies. The role is experienced differently according to gender. In spite of the fact that causes of infertility are distributed equally between the sexes, initial emphasis falls usually upon the woman.

There will be some people who have 'always known' they would not be able to have a child; nevertheless they may only just be realising how this feels. For others the truth may dawn slowly over time; but for the majority of people undergoing investigation, diagnosis comes as a bolt from the blue. They find themselves plunging head over heels into a crisis of some magnitude—'a medical condition but an emotional state'. Another key point where counselling may be sought.

The chances of their being given the diagnosis both clearly and sensitively are low—they would be quite exceptionally fortunate if both these conditions apply. Some patients receive this information in a corridor in the presence of whoever is passing, some learn indirectly when no further appointments are offered or when treatment is suggested. It is quite common for staff to deal with one partner only while the other maintains a 3 hour vigil in outpatients.

In any case, anxiety impedes the patient's acceptance of the information and understanding of the options available—most people admit to being half way down the road or back at home before their new situation sinks in. Yet the next hospital appointment offered may turn out to be months away.

The losses of infertility

Whatever the proposition: treatment, further investigations, 'wait and see', back to the GP, uncertainty is rife, the couple have crossed the bridge, they have lost their innocence; they are different, infertile, and they face a specific range of losses:

Self-esteem

For now they are flawed, unable to achieve this 'ordinary' happening which can be managed by everyone else, even the cat. They are failures in life's driving test which others pass first time round. Suddenly the population is divided into those who can and those who can't—in their distress they cannot imagine it may be difficult for others as well.

Their relationship (real)

When they came together they did not foresee this—that each would have to help and support the other (or isolate themselves from the other), through pain and disappointment. They assumed that just as they worked hard for somewhere to live, washing machine or car, so they could also work hard and become parents. Every aspect of their relationship is changed by this discovery.

Blame and anger are involved but who blames whom and is the anger appropriate? Is it clear that there is a 'fault' somewhere. Partners can go to complicated lengths to suppress blame or direct it elsewhere—each tries to compensate the other and in so doing constructs a double helix of criticism, unconscious and unrecognised, that may require much openness, sensitivity and honesty to disentangle. The counsellor as third party may be essential here to enable each to say things and hear them in a safe setting.

Their relationship (imagined)
Part of being together and hoping for a family involved projection into an imagined joint future. Each saw the other as a parent, each believed this was the person they wanted to parent with.

Confidence / Security
"If this has gone wrong, what else will go wrong?" Doubts about other parts of their lives begin to creep in—nothing is spared: work, housing, leisure, holidays, other relationships. Decisions in all these areas may have to go on hold.

Health
To be infertile is not to be ill but the treatments, drugs, regular investigations, the full acceptance of the patient role, can produce a real or imagined effect on health, outwardly 'nothing to do' with the infertility. It is not unusual for people to suffer from other illnesses which lower morale still further.

Status: 'Pronatalism' has already been mentioned. It is 'expected' that a couple will become a 'family' by the addition of children. They will provide their parents with grandchildren, falling into line with peers by becoming parents at about the same time. Ingrained in us all is the belief that we have a right and a duty to have children. Hence the equation: infertile = barren = unproductive member of society. Taking a sociological perspective, the infertile are deviant because they have not fulfilled a very basic norm.

For people who fulfil their role as parents notch up a series of rewards. They join the club—it may be only at the school gate or the supermarket check-out, but they have achieved a new status and the power that goes with it. As a further irony there are subtle punishments and implied stigma for the childless; they don't entirely belong. Moreover, whatever their story, the childfree are envied, presumed to be carefree.

Hope
A stake in the future has vanished, a chance to pass characteristics and knowledge down, to watch one's children reach adulthood, to know one

has created a new generation, secured the lineage. Hope brings a sense of purpose, a reason for staying alive and making things work. There is also the hope of being cared for in old age—implicit, but present.

Other relationships (real or imagined) are somehow diminished: with parents, friends, family, teachers, health visitors, colleagues who would have had some share in the family thus created. This may be accompanied by real losses in the here and now, as friends and family withdraw from the infertile party. Perhaps they can't cope with the couple's pain or face the difficulties created by the change in the infertile pair. (See below)

The sexual relationship

'Be fruitful and multiply'—whether a couple are taking precautions or not this is somewhere at the back of their minds. They may have waited patiently until other tasks were fulfilled, perhaps they began to 'try' for a child straight away—either way the child should have been an added expression of their love and enjoyment. Now even the best seems a 'waste'—their sex life has been purposeless. A sudden withdrawal of desire may ensue but there may be fantasy that things could be different with a different partner.

To add insult to injury, if they are going through an investigation they have to go against the grain by performing to order—on dates dictated by ovulation—grimly indicated by tedious daily temperature charts; even worse, on a date selected by the hospital for a post-coital test—rushing to the hospital in a fixed time following intercourse. Their intimate relationship, exposed to the searching eye of the medical profession, takes a turn for the worse. They feel judged—"Is twice a week normal?"

Reactions

Shock, denial, isolation, anger, guilt, depression... resembling the stages of bereavement—acceptance and resolution seem far away. It is not the same as suffering a bereavement, for there is no body to mourn and no recognised ritual. The world takes no account of their state, which may indeed be kept secret. Both we and they need reminding that the spectrum of reactions expressed and felt are perfectly normal, painful though they may be. It is only when one or two reactions occur to excess or when the individual becomes 'stuck' over months or years that pathology may be present.

A linear sequence can't do justice to the peaks and troughs involved—individuals can be appalled and bewildered at the range of feelings washing over them, each feeling further isolated because a partner suffers differently on a different timescale. There can be acute phases of extreme intensity, followed by some sort of remission or period of temporary acceptance and adjustment. Since the infertile are not ill, they still have to cope with ordinary workday demands and put on a brave face. Work may suffer seriously.

This may be a good time for counselling, the client is very vulnerable, but feelings are near the surface. If treatment is going on, most people have a great fear of ventilating their feelings in the medical setting in case they are judged unsuitable for a demanding programme like IVF or DI. It's also a time for other problems to come to the surface which have previously been blocked off or contained. Again the material uncovered may drive a client to seek independent counselling.

Rage
This comes to the surface at the injustice of it all but where can this rage be directed? A suitable target is anything or anybody that could remotely be to 'blame': parents, medical personnel past or present, God (whether or not the client has any religious beliefs), people who produce children 'as easily as falling off a log', one-parent families, the partner, oneself.

Rage introjected can manifest as paranoia, directed inwards it may turn to depression. It may find a healthy expression in action, physical activity or harmless outbursts, or it may culminate in destructive behaviour. Suppressed rage peaks in outbursts which surprise the client as much as everybody else. It may be fed by the real frustrations and inadequacies of the health service or by a mix of real and imagined failings.

Guilt
In this situation, guilt goes hand in hand with loss of self-esteem. "I am not good enough to produce a child... why?"—"Because..." and guilt spirals downwards to despair. Since we all have things to be guilty about, a reason is easy to find. Of course, past actions may appear to be relevant: a termination, a child placed for adoption, extra-marital affair, experience of rape or abuse, 'taking the pill too long', secrets from present partner.

Difficult feelings towards the partner, friends and family simply feed into this flood of self-criticism. "I'm not good enough to bear his child because I don't really love him" or "I didn't want a baby two years ago, now it's too late". Self-acceptance may be one of the richest rewards of counselling.

Isolation

This is a crisis most outsiders don't comprehend. It's likely too that many members of the sufferers' families and peer group are busy producing children. There is nobody to talk to; a cycle of withdrawal comes into being where a couple actively detach themselves from former associates who in their turn withdraw from them. "We dreaded telling them his sister was expecting her third"—colleagues at work hesitate to mention pregnancies, spontaneity gets lost. Alternatively, too much discussion of pregnancy or toddler troubles becomes almost unbearable to the infertile colleague who silently opts out.

Feelings of isolation and being different are increased by media emphasis on happy families.

Envy

Isolation turns normal generous impulses sour. It is very common for intense, unpleasant emotions to appear 'out of the blue'—a loathing of anything to do with pregnancy and childbirth, jealousy towards those who have children 'like falling off a log', 'breeding like rabbits', morbid fantasies about single parents and the sex lives of others, heavy criticism of the lifestyles and parenting abilities of others. Such feelings may provide temporary consolation but many people are bewildered that they can appear at all.

What follows is a complex distortion of peer-group and family relationships, just at a time when these are most needed. Individuals also feel they have failed their own parents in the most basic sense by not providing them with grandchildren. Existing relationship problems (sibling rivalry for instance) take on a new lease of life, intensified by the infertility problem.

What the counsellor is likely to see is a peaking of one or two of these issues in single sessions—no logical sequence here.

Envy and jealousy also extends to the very people who share the same difficulties. Far from supporting each other, the infertile may feel threatened by differences in the situations of their fellow patients: "It's different for her, she keeps on miscarrying; at least she knows she can get pregnant." support groups clinics set up for their own patients must contain an element of this, though it may be masked by niceness or surges of fund-raising.

Childishness and regression

It is ironic that the longing for a child can in itself lead to childish behaviour, almost as though the sufferers can no longer cope with adult life. One partner may seek to parent or be parented by the other, not in a spirit of play but in a desperate unconscious attempt to create a child by any means: tantrums, sulks, food fads, baby-talk, mountains of fluffy toys, exaggerated immersion in the lives of pets, excessive dependency between partners.

Obsessional behaviour

Obsessional behaviour, paranoid thoughts or actions (spying on the neighbours to find out if they are 'really married')—these states can get a grip and add to the isolation already experienced. Such behaviour is also extremely tiring and time-consuming.

Magic

Magic, handmaiden of guilt, can also claim its victims: "I've been bad but if I say these words, wear these clothes, abstain from doubt... things will be alright". "Perhaps if my mother dies/my sister loses her baby, I will conceive". Women undergoing assisted conception procedures sometimes feel a need for spells and rituals, wearing the same clothes, travelling by the same route on the clinic day. This sort of magic thinking needs verbalising in the accepting presence of the counsellor in order that the client may acknowledge its force and remain in touch with reality.

Physical reactions

It is hard for most people to acknowledge 'I am ill/tired/had this accident because I am upset.' We find another reason or become further upset, seeing the symptom as evidence of a serious illness—cancer, heart disease, stomach ulcer. Most people ignore the mind-body tie-up when it relates to themselves.

Even when the ordeal of childlessness is not accompanied by stressful investigations and treatment, grief can take a physical form—familiar enough to the bereaved: sleeplessness, loss of appetite, comfort eating, tension, tiredness, irritability, a catalogue of symptoms ranging from sore throat to athletes foot. These may take them to the doctor with disturbing frequency, the high anxiety level being disproportionate to the symptoms experienced.

Loss of libido

Loss of libido is an almost inevitable outcome of this process, whether or not treatment and medication are involved. Even the most minimal investigations are almost unbearably intrusive. If a couple are being required to 'perform to order' to maximise chances of pregnancy or to produce a post-coital test, or if they just feel a loss of purpose in their sexual relationship, 'going off sex' adds to the distress. In fact the general erosion of their relationship is a common reason for the decision to pull out of treatment.

And the loss of libido may come about at a time when they are having difficulty in telling each other how they feel and also going through vulnerability and isolation as a couple—since the rest of the world appears to be exploring and enjoying sex to the maximum—at least if the media are to be believed.

Relationship with the clinic

If treatment is involved not surprisingly the relationship with the hospital or clinic and its staff is a complex one. Attachment and dependency, with all that these imply, contain elements of ambivalence that cannot be let out in the wrong quarter. It's essential to appear well-balanced and coping for fear that treatment may be stopped. Perhaps staff will notice the level of stress and advise a six-month rest from treatment.

It can be particularly difficult for a client to insist on or even recognise their own rights within the treatment setting. These include: an adequate diagnosis with clear explanation, counselling, full information about the effects of treatment, side effects and probably outcomes, time to think, the right to refuse to participate in research. They may be asked to donate spare gametes of embryos without a chance to look at the implications. When people feel their bodies have been literally taken over, support to detach themselves from the take-over and act assertively has to come from a skilled outsider.

If the clinic is a private one, it is likely that the material conditions and level of privacy will be to a high standard but costs to the client may equal the price of a small car. If treatment occurs within the NHS a woman may find herself on the same ward as patients undergoing abortion and sterilisation. Investigations may be pursued on premises normally occupied by the antenatal clinic. In either setting the opportunities for healthy grumbling and protest are nipped in the bud by the need to appear grateful and conforming.

An individual undergoing treatment may long to verbalise doubts and questions, but feel obliged to hold back. They may find procedures hard to understand or so demanding that their life is completely taken over. But there is a strong need to 'please' at all costs. How can the patient express the normal healthy fears which accompany an important life change? "I'm afraid of childbirth"..."Will I be a good parent?", "Will my child be the right sex?"

It is even less likely that patients will feel safe enough or find the words to bring out fantasies concerning bodily events, eggs and embryos in storage, donors and semen—that is if these fantasies are conscious. For the treatment culture is mechanical, however sympathetic the staff, and patients believe they must remain compliant throughout the procedures. Fantasies hidden from the individual may find expression in dreams, 'surprise' behaviour, daydreaming, inexplicable fears.

So how can the individual, well-ensconced in the patient role, continually look realistically at their changes of success? After all they have to keep their hopes high in order to maintain commitment to a gruelling programme of medication and intervention (even where percentages quoted for their form of treatment are dismally low). When it comes to stopping treatment the couple may want others to decide for them.

Understandably the medical staff are not usually equipped to help patients explore mixed feelings. Clinics are geared to successful treatment and to research within the field of human embryology and fertilisation. Their goals include improving take-home baby figures and continually evolving effective new ways of working. Support groups do exist for those undergoing specific treatment. The waiting room may include an attractive noticeboard with details of events and photographs of babies and children.

When treatment ends in failure and disappointment, good models of the child-free lifestyle are not usually available, either explicitly or implicitly. Helping people to 'let go' and decide 'enough is enough' is not usually within the medical brief. If qualified counselling comes within the service, the counsellor may have managed to help the client hold this possibility in mind from the beginning, so moving forward, though painful, may not bring such devastation.

If treatment fails, a couple find themselves faced with the loss of an intense relationship with the clinic which may have lasted years. Besides losing the hope of a child, they seem to have 'failed' strong parent-figures to whom they owed considerable loyalty—or have the parent figures abandoned them? These factors can be influential in decisions to carry on with treatment.

Society's view

The infertile are at the receiving end of much insensitivity, whether their situation is understood or not. "You can have my kids any time", "Enjoy yourselves, kids aren't all they're cracked up to be". Good advice: "Just relax, it'll happen"—admonitions to adopt, or take a holiday. Such advice is as likely to come from figures in authority as from the next door neighbour. Hospitals and doctors justify the low priority given to the problem with the words "You don't die of infertility, after all".

But alternatively, stopping treatment can lose support from family and friends. 'Try, try, try again' is the ethos, and their plight is likened to cousins who had trouble selling their house or a sister who persevered until she got promotion.

All this has the effect of denying true feelings any expression. The infertile have to learn a bland 'cover story' for public use which fends off intrusive questions.

It doesn't help that there is regular media focus on children and 'the family'. Public debate about infertility, causes, treatment and research, tends to focus on the embryo, on 'ethical' issues; e.g. use of eggs from foetuses, not on the feelings of individuals or of children who may result.

There are additional stresses in a multi-cultural society for those whose cultural roots lie elsewhere. Motivations may vary and cause different reactions to diagnosis and the search for treatment.

Traditionalists from Asian and Muslim cultures may deny the existence of male infertility, so testing applies to the female partner only. If she is labelled barren, the only possible outcome may be divorce. On the other hand the shock, disgrace and humiliation for a man from a male-dominated culture who agrees to be tested and is diagnosed infertile may be all the more intense because it is an experience not previously recognised by his cultural group.

The practice of in-family adoption which appeared to work well as a 'solution' for childless couples in their country of origin can fall foul of what may be seen as the 'red tape' of British adoption legislation.

While the couple seeking help may appear 'Westernised', having grown up and been educated in this country, they may be coping with pressure or incomprehension from an extended family with more traditional views and experiences.

Different cultures create different pressures—in some the birth of a male child is as crucial as fertility itself, in others marriage may not be considered before a woman has 'proved herself fertile'. For some women from African or Middle Eastern backgrounds, it may have been female circumcision which has rendered them unable to produce a child.

The pursuit of happiness

People believe they have a right to have children. When this right appears to be threatened it becomes dominant and children are seen as the key to happiness, like falling in love. Cultures hold their own interpretations of the myth of the 'magic child' whose birth restores balance to humanity. We know myths speak in a universal voice to us all but it is dangerous indeed to confuse symbol and actuality. 'Cat's cradle of hopes can hold no living baby.'

'Trying' for a baby can be a way of avoiding, delaying or hoping to solve other personal problems which have been put on hold. This can lead to over-emphasis on the child as solution.

Even when this is not the case, pursuing the quest beyond healthy limits skews other life tasks and places a heavy burden on the shoulders of any child eventually conceived. Parents whose children were adopted or born as a result of assisted conception still live with the disappointment that this was not quite the child they wanted.

If this can be accepted and expressed, ordinary healthy ambivalence has replaced problem-solving magic. If parents maintain the impossible dream that a child will take away their pain, they won't be able to meet the needs of an ordinary, fallible human child and the family is at risk.

Adoption
Medical personnel are not always au fait with the current adoption scene. Adoption tends to get a bad press and is still perceived by the man in the street as a way of meeting the needs of childless couples. So it is a particularly painful discovery for would-be adopters when they learn that the goal of adoption agencies is to meet the needs of children in care. It demands a change of focus for which they may be

emotionally unprepared. If they are seeing a counsellor who can support them in throwing the necessary internal switches they will be spared some bruises.

In fact the position regarding the sort of children who need adoption, together with the requirements of adoption agencies, is changing all the time (almost as rapidly as infertility treatments). Agencies work within adoption legislation which is regularly revised. In addition, each agency has policies specific to itself regarding the sort of adopters they need and are happy to take on. This will include such factors as: age, whether or not married, single parents, sexual orientation, etc. They vary enormously and it is important for possible applicants to sound out several to get a clear picture of their requirements.

When treatment fails or when there is no medical solution anyway, consultants and GPs advise adoption. It is not their field and the advice is given in good faith. When friends and family advise adoption there can be an element of folk-medicine in their private hope that an adopted child will somehow make the couple fertile. It is hard not to go along with this. There is still a picture somewhere of a baby arriving who will be like the couple's own child. Nothing could be further from the truth. It would be extremely helpful if accurate, up to date information about adoption could be available to infertile couples well before it becomes their only option, so that their thinking ahead can be based on the realities rather than the dream.

Adoption agencies are child-focused—they have in their care children who are unable, for serious reasons, to return to their natural parents. A long period of assessment and formal decision making has preceded this. There may have been failed attempts to restore children to their own parents and many children are in care for several years before the adoption decision is reached.

So adoption agencies (voluntary and Local Authority) are looking for families who can parent wounded children but still help each growing child to understand something of its roots and the reasons it can't go home. Contact between an adopted child and members of his birth family is increasingly part of the contract. Certainly adopters are expected to demonstrate an accepting attitude to the first family and be open with the child.

People considering adoption can be shocked by the sudden change of emphasis. They may have been immersed in their own needs over a long period—now they are being asked to put themselves in the shoes of a child who has suffered early trauma followed by a series of moves in care. Some people may not feel ready to make this leap of the imagination or feel it is too high a price to pay when they are still licking their wounds. It is sometimes easier for one partner than the other.

An adoption application will take a long time, many agencies have waiting lists, even pre-assessments—most will only take up applications which match the children waiting (so if they have only over-fives to place, they won't take to the starting post people who want under-fives).

Once again, infertile people find themselves heavily dependent on an organisation which has the power to provide them with a child. The assessment, by one or two social workers, will be searching, exploring childhood, developmental history, past and present relationships. There will be a very thorough medical (though Agency policies vary about medical requirements). The social worker will want to know if the couple are receiving counselling elsewhere.

An adoption application also involves a police check. There is usually a group training programme which aims at helping adopters to understand the effects of separation and loss, looking at the implications of adoption. The sense of rage and unfairness often bites deep at this time, as adopters learn the reasons why children had to be removed from birth parents. It brings home the irony for themselves of having to be assessed to be 'good enough' for what others 'don't even deserve'. But they also learn of the birth parents' grief at parting with their children and this is an area for mixed feelings.

If an atmosphere of honesty and good partnership prevails, all this can be both healing and constructive but some would-be adopters find it intrusive. They dread rejection and if this comes it can be deeply destructive. Acceptance too brings an awe-inspiring awareness of the task ahead, ambivalence is natural. Sometimes acceptance on to an adoption waiting list leads to the break-up of a relationship—too much reality.

Being introduced to a child, getting to know them and their past history, understanding their pain and how this may come out over the years, integrating them into the household, is a testing time for individuals who may feel their own relationship eroded by what has gone before.

Adoption, like infertility, is a life-long condition and this takes slow learning. With the placement of more difficult and damaged children for adoption, and greater understanding of the life-long needs of all parties to the 'adoption triangle'—birth parents, adoptive parents and adoptees —many areas now have independent post-adoption services free of involvement from any specific agency, which provide counselling, advice and help to all parties to adoption at any stage in their lives.

Fostering

This is rarely a suitable option for individuals without children of their own who are longing to become parents. I mention it because it sometimes gets confused with adoption. Fostering implies shared care where links with the natural family are still retained if possible and where the Local Authority retains ultimate responsibility. The plan may be for the child to return home eventually or to move to adoptive parents. Older children who need long-term fostering are often deeply troubled youngsters with traumatic life experiences.

Resolution

How much can this really happen? The crisis may have lasted 3 months, 3 years or 15 years, and the acute phase subsides with time. Healing cannot mean total recovery and there is no ritual for the childless. A counsellor may find themselves confronted by a client in her 70s for whom the issue has peaked again, triggered by more immediate difficulties; feelings re-emerge from 30 years cold storage fresh as the day they were first experienced.

At whatever stage client and counsellor come together, and whatever the immediate issues, a steady, realistic, plodding part of the work has to be directed towards acceptance: acknowledging the loss, letting go of blame, re-channelling parenting energies, embracing the search for wholeness and looking at options for a fulfilling childfree life.

At a societal level, I wonder what we can all do to challenge the norm, placing more value on the role childless people play in society and on the quality of life without children—it takes courage and a regular questioning of our own assumptions. If parenting was genuinely not regarded as an absolute right and duty, more people might feel confident to ask "Should I have children?"

Resources

ISSUE (formerly National Association for the Childless)
509 Aldridge Road, Great Barr, Birmingham B44 8NA. Tel: 021-344 4414
National organisation with regional network. Quarterly magazine and very useful, clear, up to date factsheets (members only) on all main causes of infertility. plus list of books and tapes available by post. Issue continually campaigns for improvement and greater availability of treatment. Very supportive for individuals undergoing treatment. Not really relevant for those trying to come to terms with childlessness.

CHILD
PO Box 154, Hounslow, Middlesex TW5 0EZ.   Tel: 0181-571 4367
Very similar to ISSUE, with magazine and factsheets for members.

RELATE (National Marriage Guidance Council)
Herbert Gray College, Little Church Street, Rugby, Warwickshire CV21 3AP.
                                                      Tel: 01788 573241
Local Relate offices to be found in telephone directory.
Useful bookshop, booklist available: relationships and psychosexual problems. Books can be ordered by post.

FORESIGHT (Association for the Promotion of Pre-conception Care)
The Old Vicarage, Church Lane, Whitley, Godalming, Surrey GU8 5PN.
                                                      Tel: 01728 794500
Aims to look at client as a whole, advice regarding diet, allergies, healthy lifestyle, etc, in preparation for conception.

SANDS (Stillbirth & Neonatal Death Society)
28 Portland Place, London W1N 4DE.   Tel: 0171-436 5881
For parents whose babies are born dead or die soon after birth.

TAMBA (Twins & Multiple Births Association)
For parents who have lost one or both twins or babies from a multiple birth.
Contact through SANDS.

MA (Miscarriage Association)
PO Box 24, Ossett, West Yorkshire WF5 9SG. Tel: 01924 830515 (ansaphone)
For parents who have experienced miscarriage.

SAFTA (Support After Termination for Abnormality)
29-30 Soho Square, London W1V 6JB.   Tel: 1071-439 6124

COTS (Childlessness Overcome Through Surrogacy)
Loandhu Cottage, Gruids, Lairg, Sutherland, Scotland.   Tel: 01549 2401

Endometriosis Self-Help Group
65 Holmdene Avenue, Herne Hill, London SE24 9LD.   Tel: 0181-659 3368

Support networks for women who have undergone or are contemplating reconstructive vaginal surgery

London Network:
Hilary Everett, Gynaecological Social Worker Social Services Department, St. Bartholomew's Hospital, West Smithfield, London EC1A 7BE.
Tel: 0171-601 8718
Putting adults in touch with each other.

Northern Network:
Sheila Naish, 35 Royd Terrace, Hebden Bridge, West Yorkshire HX7 7BT.
Tel: 01422 845304
Putting adults in touch with each other. Occasional support meetings.

AIS (Androgen Insensitivity Syndrome) Support Group
Jackie Burrows, 2 Shirburn Avenue, Mansfield, Nottinghamshire NG18 2BY.
Tel: 01623 661749
Telephone support and advice to adults with AIS and parents of affected children. The syndrome (formerly known as Testicular Feminisation Syndrome) occurs when a male foetus develops a female body due to a rare inherited insensitivity to male hormones. Factsheet and articles available.

BAAF (British Agencies for Adoption & Fostering)
Skyline House, 200 Union Street, London SE1 0LY.   Tel: 0171-593 2000
Also some regional offices. Wide list of publications for adults and children including list of current adoption agencies throughout UK and their requirements.

PPIAS (Parent to Parent Information on Adoption Services)
Philly Morrall, PPIAS, Lower Boddington, Daventry,
Northamptonshire NN11 6YB.   Tel: 01327 60295
An organisation run by adoptive parents aims to help other potential adoptive families by passing on information about how and where to apply. Quarterly newsletter — well written and excellent value.

Overseas Adoption Helpline
First floor, 34 Upper Street, London N1 0PN.   Tel: 0171-226 7666
Advice and information to prospective adopters

BICA (British Infertility Counselling Association)
Membership Secretary, Trish Chandler, The White House, High Street, Campsall, Doncaster DN6 9AF.
Organisation founded in 1990. Organisational member of BAC. National with regional groups. Regular seminars, study days and informal meetings. Quarterly newsletter.

Reading List

Books for Clients

The Infertility Handbook	Sarah J. Biggs (Fertility Services Management, Gloucestershire GL6 7RL)
Infertility	Roger Neuberg (Thorsons)
Resource Directory	Irene Tubbs (Irene Tubbs, 26 Overmead, Sidcup, Kent DA15 8DS). Clinical services, treatments, support networks and infertility counselling—mostly in the south east, basic practical advice.
Getting Pregnant	R. Winston (Anaya)
Never to be a Mother	Linda Hunt Anton (Harper Collins). Self-help book and guide for all women who couldn't have children. Ten steps to healing the heartache and leading a rich, childfree life.
The Gift of a Child	R & E Snowden (University of Exeter Press)
The Well Woman's Self Help Directory	Nicki Bradford (Sidgwick & Jackson)
Family	Susan Hill (Michael Joseph). Sensitive novel, theme of which is premature birth and miscarriage.
Miscarriage	Christine Moulder (Pandora)
Miscarriage	Ann Oakley, Ann McPherson & Helen Roberts (Penguin)
Hidden Loss	V. Hey (Women's Press)
Infertility, Stress & Anxiety	S. Jennings (Blackwell Scientific)
My Story	Book by two mothers of children conceived by donor insemination intended as a means of introducing the child's origins to the child (The Infertility Research Trust, Dept of Obs & Gynae, Jessop Hospital for Women, Leavygreave Road, Sheffield S3 7RE).

Tapes and videos to help people decide on IVF or Donor Insemination treatment (HFEA, Paxton House, 30 Artillery Lane, London E1 7LS).

Books for Counsellors

Human Fertilisation & Embryology Act 1990	(HMSO)
Blackstones Guide to the HFE Act	Morgan & Lee (Blackstone Press)
Warnock Report, 1984	(HMSO)
HFE Authority	[Annual Reports, tapes and videos] (Paxton House, 30 Artillery Lane, London E1 7LS)
Counselling for Regulated Treatments	— Report of the King's Fund Centre Counselling Committee 1991
British Infertility Counselling Association	—bibliography available from: Liz Latarche, ACU Dept., BUPA Hospital, The Old Watton Road, Colney, Norwich NR4 7TD.
Childless No Choice	James Monach (Routledge)
An Approach to Community Mental Health	G. Caplan (Tavistock)
Why Children?	S. Dowrick & S. Grundberg (Women's Press)
The Presentation of Self in Everyday Life	E. Goffman (Penguin)
Stigma	E. Goffman (Prentice Hall)
Unfocused Grief	P & D Houghton (Issue)
Infertility (Modern Treatments)	M Jones (Piatkus)
Bereavement	Murray Parkes (Tavistock)
The Artificial Family	R Snowden & D Mitchell (George Allen & Unwin). Artificial insemination.
Psychological Processes of Childbearing	J. Raphael Leff (Chapman Hall)
Infertility: A Guide for the Childless Couple	B.E. Menning (Prentice Hall)
Childhood & Society	E. Erikson (Penguin)
Passages	G. Sheehy (Bantam)
The Making & Breaking of Affectional Bonds	J. Bowlby (Routledge)
Gestalt Counselling Skills in Action	P. Clarkson (Sage)
Stress Protection Plan	L. Chaitow (Thorsons)
Male Infertility: Men Talking	Mary Claire Mason (Routledge)
The Dreamwork Manual	S. Kaplan-Williams (Aquarian Press)

The Psychosocial Needs of Semen Donors	K.R. Daniels in Reproduction Life by Wijma & von Schoultz, eds. (Carnforth, Parthenon)
Infertility Counselling: The Need for a Psycho-Social Perspective	Ken Daniels (British Journal of Social Work 1993, 23, pp 501-515)
The Baby Makers: An In-Depth Study of Psychological Reactions to Infertility & Baby-Making Technology	J. Raphael Leff (British Journal of Psychotherapy, Vol 8, No 3, pp 92)
Once a Dark Secret	Anon (BMJ 19.2.94). A personal experience of testicular feminisation. Letters in response, BMJ 16.4.94.
Does she need to know she is a he?	Dr. E. Scott (GP 19.2.93). Discusses testicular feminisation
Infertility & Adoption	Burnell, Reich & Sawbridge (Post Adoption Centre, 8 Torriano Mews, Torriano Avenue, London NW5 2RZ)
The Stork & the Syringe: A political history of reproductive medicine	Naomi Pfeffer (Polity Press)

References

The figures for Chapter One[†] come in part from Sarah Biggs *The Infertility Handbook* and from a paper given by Robin Yates to a BAAF Seminar on infertility.

These are largely estimates as there has been surprisingly little data collected nationally.

Monach cites Rachootin & Olsen in Denmark 1981 found 9% of women failed to conceive during 2 years of trying. A recent survey in the West Country (Hull et al) estimated that 1 in 6 couples needed infertility help or treatment